G000123474

The Good Life in in Galicia

www.CyberworldPublishing.com

This book is copyright © S Bush 2016
First published by Cyberworld Publishing in 2016
Cover design: Copyright Cyberworld Publishing 2016
Cover photo: manipulated, Copyright: S. Bush 2016
Photos of "La Gorda", window shutter, and seat: Copyright: J
Suffolk
All photos in "Vendimia in the Ribeira Sacra of Galicia":
Copyright: Stephen Bush
E-book ISBN: 978-0-9953873-2-4
Paperback ISBN: 978-0-9953873-4-8
All rights reserved

No part of this book may be reproduced in any form,
except for the inclusion of brief quotations in a review or
article, without written permission from the author or
publisher.

~

Cyberworld Publishing
www.cyberworldpublishing.com

The Good Life in Galicia

An Anthology

Edited by S. Bush

Contents

Introduction

This anthology began as an idea for a competition to encourage people to write about Galicia and raise awareness of this fascinating part of Green Spain. As we are an English-language publisher the stories had to be in English, and to make it easy, entrants did not have to have lived in Galicia or to have even visited here.

There were two outstanding contest entries—one in each category, fortunately, and they form the core of this anthology. "A Country Is More than Lines on a Map" by Robin Hillard, an Australian who has never been to Galicia, except on the Net, was the fiction winner, and her story is a Romance of many layers. "La Gorda and the Asociacion Autocaravanistas de Galicia," by Galician resident J. P. Vincent, was the nonfiction winner and gives us a humorous look at how events, like a visit from the police, can change our lives.

The rest of the anthology comprises works written by well-known authors who were invited to submit specially written pieces, or in the case of Eddie Rock, to allow us to use an excerpt from his book *The Camino de Santiago: A Sinners Guide*.

In "Jesus Speaks Galician," best-selling author Olivia Stowe has produced a homage to the importance of family and the openness of the Galician people. Steve Kessel has produced a foreigner's view of Galicia in an almost Romance, and there are also poems, a recipe, and a story of the vineyards. The vines being an integral part of Galician life.

We hope you enjoy this brief look at an ancient land, one full of generous people and natural splendours, and agree that there is indeed a lot of good in a life in Galicia.

~

Recipe: Galician Sopa de Calabacin

by Stephen Bush

This year my vegetable garden (huerta) has produced an overabundance of zucchini (calabacin), and I have been busy making soup and freezing it for the winter. This recipe came from a woman I met in the local village shop, but she added some olive oil (aciete de olivia) to it. I prefer it without the oil.

Galician Sopa de Calabacina
Galician Zucchini/Courgette Soup

Ingredients:
(Preferably all vegetables are fresh from your vegetable garden (huerta), and the quantities and variety of ingredients used will depend mainly on what you have harvested on the day or have in your barn, or fridge.)

Zucchini (calabacin)
Onions (cebollas)
Leeks (puerros)
Potatoes (patatas)
Chicken stock (caldo de pollo) made from real chickens and vegetables

Spring water (agua de manantiel) from a local spring (font), if needed

A large pot for cooking the soup in.

Preparation:
If the zucchini are small, just slice; if very large, like marrows, you may need to skin them and possibly deseed them before slicing.
Peel and chop the onions.
Clean and slice the leeks and discard the hard tops.
Peel and slice the potatoes.

Place alternating layers of potato, onion, zucchini, and leek in a large pot and just cover with the chicken stock or a mix of the chicken stock and spring water.

Bring the soup to the boil and simmer gently until all ingredients are soft. Remove from stove and prepare to serve. May be served mashed, pureed, or in natural lumps.

Serve with chorizo (preferably locally made) slices, traditional bread, a Galician wine, and good company.

Enjoy.

~

Winner of First Prize, for fiction, in "The Good life in Galicia" short story competition 2016

A Country Is More than Lines on a Map

by Robin Hillard

"You've got a lovely position here," Jacqui said, walking to my big window and gazing at the land that stretched below the downward sweep of my garden. "It's nearly as good as Galicia," she added, laughing as she quoted her grandmother.

I laughed with her. The words took me back many years, away from my Queensland home and across a continent, to a hot dry goldfields town in Western Australia, where my six-year-old self sat in Josefina's kitchen, listening to stories about green, rainy Galicia. "Nearly as good as Galicia." Those words had been her highest praise for anything she admired in her new country.

Galicia! We children knew there was no such place. We stopped believing in Galicia when we learned it was Dad, not Father Christmas, who put the presents in our stockings on Christmas Eve. And Mum, not the tooth fairy, who spirited away our teeth, leaving sixpenny bits in their place.

But we loved Josefina's stories about a land of enchantments, where magical beings guarded fantastic

11

treasure and beautiful mouras cast their spells on unwary travellers.

When we were older, our views changed again. We knew Galicia was as real as the bicycles that came on Christmas morning, or Mum's footsteps when she tiptoed into our bedroom to trade coins for our teeth. Dad showed us the word *"Galicia"* in his big atlas, on a page marked *"SPAIN,"* so we were puzzled when Josefina received news of her people in an envelope with Argentinean stamps.

"In bad times people left their homes to find work overseas," Josefina explained, as she stirred a pot of her special pork-and-potato soup. "Most of them went to South America. But their hearts stayed Galicia. And now the government wants us all to use Castilian Spanish, so our ways, and our language are dying in Spain and it is the traballadores estraxeiros who keep the Galician ways alive. One day, little Betsy, you will learn that a country is more than lines on a map." That was over fifty years ago, and today Josefina's granddaughter is sitting in my Queensland kitchen talking about Galicia. But this is a Galicia with its own regional parliament and a language recognised in official documents, and where the fascinating "Galician ways," which were so much part of Josefina's stories, are practised with joyful pride.

"Did you go to Spain?" Jacqui asked.

I shook my head. I had done my travelling in the early sixties, when Franco was still in power, and although his government welcomed the tourist pound, I would not go to his country. Because there was one afternoon I would never forget, just before Jacqui's mother was born.

My brothers were at school, but I was home with a cold, when Josefina came, as she often did, to talk to Mum. The women passed through the sitting room where I was settled in a big armchair, but she did not notice me as they moved into the kitchen.

Mum put the kettle on, and while she continued shelling peas, they talked about the coming baby. If she was

12

a girl she was to be called Rosalia, "after Rosalia de Castro," Josefina explained. "She was the greatest poet in all Galicia. She wrote in our own Galego language, and her poetry gave it new power."

She sang a trill of strange, magical sounds, paused and repeated the tune in words I could understand.

I will sing about you, Galicia
Beside the fountains,
For so they asked me,
For so they bade me
That I should sing and sing
In the language I speak,
For so they bade me
For so they told me.

"And if the baby is a boy, what will you call him?" mum asked.

"Eduardo, after my poor dead father. They killed him. Because he was Republican."

What was a Republican? I wondered, straining to hear more.

"One evening a crowd of neighbours came to our house, screaming his name. They broke down the door with their axes and dragged him away. We never saw him again."

Josefina started to cry and Mum murmured sympathy while I sat, still as a frightened mouse, wondering what it would be like to have neighbours break into your home.

"They said he killed a priest," Josefina continued, answering Mum's soft questions. "Some of the Republican's did do dreadful things, but not my father. He was a good man. He loved Galicia.

"After any Republican was killed, the mob hounded his family. They would chase a Republican's wife in the street and sometimes they shaved the women's hair. The children were also abused."

13

I scrunched down in the chair, knowing if Josefina saw me she would stop talking, and I wanted to hear more.

Although her father was a Republican (that word again), Josefina said, her mother's family were staunch Catholics and her uncle was a priest. After her father was killed, her mother took her to her aunt's house, "where they thought I would be safe. But Aunt Maria was not happy. If the villagers learned about my father, she was afraid her family would be blamed for keeping me. She was worried about her own children. She told my uncle to get me away and he came one night, with potatoes in a cart. We drove all the way to Bilbao in the Basque country."

At the time I knew nothing about the Spanish Civil War. I did not understand the nightmare that blasted Josefina's childhood, but her story stayed with me, and over the years, as I learned some of Spanish history, I added my own embellishments.

I imagined Josefina with her uncle-priest driving that cart of potatoes across the North of Spain. When they were in Franco's territory, I thought she would take the reins, posing as a farmer's daughter. If they were stopped by Franco's men, her uncle could flaunt his priesthood and claim they were delivering food to the convent. In other areas her uncle would hide all signs of religion and drive the cart himself, claiming the girl was his daughter and telling any questioners that they were taking potatoes to the Republican fighters.

"There had been bombing in the Basque country." Josefina continued her story while Mum poured another cup of tea. "When we got to Bilbao, some ships were taking children to England. My uncle pushed me among some of the Basque girls. I crouched in a corner and pretended I was too frightened to speak because my Galician tongue would have given me away. It was an awful night. The boat was crowded and the seas were so rough and the wind so cold that all the children were sick. At last we reached England, where people were kind. They could not find my

14

mother after the war, so I stayed in England until," and I was relieved to hear the familiar, happy lilt in her voice, "I married my Michael and he brought me here to Australia. I hope my baby will be as fortunate."

Josefina never spoke of those black days again, but when teenage rebellion pitted me against my gentle father, she took me to one side and she said, "You should be grateful that you still have him." I remembered her story and was ashamed of my petulance.

That was why, when I was working in London in 1964, I would not go to Franco's Spain. But my flatmates did. And their accounts of nightclubs and sunshine on the Costa del Sol did not sound like Josefina's beloved rainy, green Galicia.

There was one place that reminded me of Josefina's stories. Ireland. Another rainy, green country where narrow roads wound through grey stone villages and rain drizzled down from cloudy skies.

In the sixties there were no digital devices to display the record of our travels. We loaded our cameras with film, and when the roll was finished, we took it to a Kodak store to be developed.

Our photos were returned in small yellow boxes of square, transparent slides. After we got home, we would gather our family and friends in a darkened room and project those slides onto a screen, while we talked about our adventures. Josefina loved my photos of Ireland, "The country is so green, so like Galicia," she said.

Jacqui showed her photos differently, on a digital device. She brushed her fingers across the surface to change the scene, and her views of the granite villages, green hills, and rocky shores of Galicia made me want to cry. My tears were not for Galicia, but for a country that, only a few years after I left, tore itself apart as Spain had done in Josefina's childhood. I thought of one journey in Northern Ireland, travelling in a small, elderly bus on a road that wound through tiny, grey stone villages. Protestant? Catholic?

Where the driver greeted children coming home from school, and women with string shopping bags chatted like old friends. What happened to them when the country exploded into violence?

How much did Jacqui know of her grandmother's story? I mentioned the Civil War.

"They still don't talk about it much," she said. "Not to outsiders. Perhaps old countries should forget the past?" Her rising tone turned the statement into a question, one I could not answer.

She swiped her screen again, to wipe the problem away. "Pilgrims on the Camino," she said, showing a crowd of young people in hiking gear under the trees in an outdoor café. "They come from all over the world to walk to the Cathedral of Santiago de Compostela. Those girls," she pointed to a trio roughly her own age, "are from Russia. those," an elderly couple, "are German, and the family sitting next to them are French. I learned to say 'hello,' in about twenty different languages." I thought that answered the earlier implied question.

"Did you know St James, the disciple, preached in Galicia?" she asked me. "After he was killed in Rome, his followers brought his body back to Galicia."

I nodded. Josefina had made that story come alive, although, as a Republican's daughter, she'd laughed during the telling. She said, as she often did at the end of her tales, "I don't believe it, but it's true."

"These are real pilgrims." Jacqui moved her fingers across the screen to show a church group walking together with what looked like a heavy cross.

"They made me feel bad," she said. "It was just a holiday for us. We spent a couple of nights in the pilgrim's hostel." She showed me a long room, crowded with beds, "but mostly we stayed in small guest houses and stopped at little cafés along the way. At least we carried our own gear. This group . . ." a happy crowd setting out with small day packs, "they had their luggage carried to their hotels. There

16

are so many phony pilgrims. What would St James think of them?"

"He'd be delighted," I said firmly. "Wasn't he a fisherman himself, and didn't he appreciate a full net? And wouldn't he have been glad of the money his family got for his fish. Why wouldn't he be happy to see young people working in those hotels, or making a few euros carting pilgrim's bags?

"Shrines and pilgrimages, they've always been about money," I told her. "Why do you think medieval churchmen stole the bodies of saints? They wanted pilgrims to come to their church, with gifts. And perhaps St James was looking into the future when he wanted his bones to lie in Galicia. Maybe he knew how much, one day, the country would need pilgrim trade. I don't believe that, but it's true," I added, making Jacqui laugh.

Her fingers brushed past pictures of the Camino to show me a rather uninteresting, square building, with a group of children gathered around a large young man. "That's a school," she said, unnecessarily, "in a village not far from A Coruna. And that's Connor. He's an American, teaching English, and he got special permission for me to visit his class. And he took me to a fiesta. Not a big one, like I saw in Santiago, but a real village celebration."

She showed me photos of more children, with their families clustered around four men, in what looked like medieval costume. "That's a fiesta band, pipes and drums. They go around all the village fiestas, playing traditional music, but they also play modern tunes. The pipes are called gaitas and you hear them everywhere.

"It was great. All Connor's students were there. And everybody was singing and dancing, even the little ones stayed till the last, late fireworks.

"And the food! Galician food is great. Empanadas, that's a kind of pie stuffed with meat or fish and Polpo a Feira, chunks of octopus served with olive oil, salt (Connor

17

always says sea-salt) and pimenton, Galician pimento. You wouldn't believe how good it is."

I laughed, remembering the way we children pulled faces when Josefina talked about the food of her homeland. It is hard to believe how insular we were, before a tide of "New Australians" showed us there was more to a good meal than potatoes and roast lamb.

"Connor shared an apartment in A Coruna, so he knew some great places to eat."

"I thought he was teaching at a village school."

"He is. But some of the teachers live in the city and he can drive to school with them."

"And you also stayed in A Coruna?"

"It was handy for sightseeing."

And for Connor. I didn't say the words aloud, but Jacqui read my mind.

"I was lucky to meet him," she said defensively. "He showed me the real Galicia and introduced me to his Galician friends. They're more reserved than the Spaniards we met in the South, but they're lovely when you get to know them."

Like Josefina. She was a wonderful friend, but she was never quite at ease in the casual hail-fellow-well-met attitude of the Western Goldfields. When I was showing my slides, I had a photo of the Irish woman I met in the glass house of the Belfast Botanic Gardens where we discovered a mutual love of palms. When I said the woman invited me to her home for afternoon tea, Josefina was shocked. Take a stranger into your home? That was not something she would ever do.

I often wondered what happened to my Belfast friend. Had she been killed in the fighting, like Jacqui's great grandfather? Or did she survive to enjoy the fragile peace?

Jacqui was still talking about Galicians. "They are always very polite. Courteous." As she shaped the old fashioned word, I thought how well it described Josefina. She was courteous.

As a child, some of her courtesies had puzzled me. Whatever Mum offered, Josefina would refuse at first, but when asked a second time she would accept.

And if she was looking after me, she'd frown when my grubby hands reached for the one remaining slice of cake. "You shouldn't take the last one," she would say. "It's not polite." (But in the kitchen afterwards, when she was putting the tea things away, she'd always give me that same piece of cake.)

Jacqui swiped her screen again. A Coruna. Herself and Connor in front of a lighthouse. "That's the Tower of Hercules. And that," Connor was dwarfed by the statue of a huge warrior, "is Breogan. He built the highest lighthouse in the world. His sons climbed to the top and saw Ireland."

That was another one of Josefina's stories. Her voice would deepen and her eyes would shine as she told us how the great chief Breogan built a great lighthouse, and how, from the top of that lighthouse, his sons saw the mountains of Ireland rising out of the mist. "So sons of Breogan sailed away to a land of honey and corn." If her husband was in the room she would beam at him and add "a country where, many years later, a boy called Michael was born."

"Of course they couldn't really see Ireland," Jacqui said, "but the Celts from Galicia did take their boats across the Atlantic. Connor's family came from Ireland, and he researched their history while he was there. That's how he learned about the sons of Breogan."

"I don't believe it, but it's true," I murmured again.

"A later generation of those Galician Celts left Ireland and settled in Scotland. They took their music with them." Jacque continued her history as she showed me another photo, a band of pipers, costumed like the musicians at the village fiesta. "Look at them. Aren't they like the Scottish highlanders? And those pipes, gaita, don't they make you think of the Scots bagpipes?"

Was that why Josefina loved our goldfields' bagpipe band, which, as Dad said, was "more or less Scottish, and very keen," though not always musical.

"Isn't it strange," Jacqui said, "here's Connor, from America, whose people left Galicia while Breogan was king, and me born in Australia with a Galician grandmother, and we leave two continents to come together—in Galicia!"

"A country is more than lines on a map," I told Josefina's granddaughter.

~

The young Josefina had a fragmented view of the Insurrection that started The Spanish Civil War. And Betsy admits her picture of the girl's flight to Bilbao has been drawn from the few words she overheard as a child. If you want to know what really happened in Galicia during those first terrible weeks, you should read "Galicia's Role in the Civil War."
richardhenricksen24.wordpress.com/2016/03/01/galicias-role-in-the-spanish-civil-war/

If you want more of Rosalia de Castro's poetry, Eduardo Freire Canosa has very generously put his translations into the public domain at http://rosaliadecastropoems.esy.es/#Poem1

~

The Galician Virus

by J. P. Vincent

"*Estoy enferma*" announced my companion at conversation
    classes.
I awoke, the next day, my throat sore and itchy.
My Galician invader had sent its first warning shot across
    the bow in bed on the first night.
A second shot was fired.
A ringing in my ears, the sound of The Antibodies in
    defence.
I can't hear, can't smell, and can't taste anything, the first
    battle goes to The Galician Virus.

My sore throat's gone, a minor success for The Antibodies.
A woolly head and the rushing thumping sounds of The
    Cavalry charge,
The Antibodies bring in their second line of defence.

Silence, my woolly head is clearing.
A tickle in my throat. I squeak, The Galician Virus has
    failed on two fronts; he's trying for a third.
The tickle is working its way onto my chest.
I move, cough, I squeak, cough, I think, cough, cough.
The Galician Virus is exploring new frontiers to attack one
    at a time.
I clutch my chest as another coughing spasm takes hold.

21

Chest aches, the coughing subsides.
Now shoulders, elbows, and knees ache.
Where are The Cavalry? Defeated or regrouping.
The new day dawns, the sun shines, clarity.
I blow my nose one last time and say goodbye to the
remnants of The Galician Virus, who fought a
valiant war.
Drop the tissue in the loo and flush his remains into the
sewers.

The winner is, the magnificent, stupendous, wonderful
Human Body.
Hurrah.

~

The Power of a Casual Word

by Steve Kessel

He looked at his friend Antonio across the table and frowned. Not at anything in particular, just because he was thinking about things and the thoughts were moving into difficult waters. He really had no idea how Antonio felt about their relationship.

"Is something wrong?" Antonio asked.

"No. Nothing," he replied, forcing a smile. "Just tired."

"So on Saturday, you want to go to A Cova, to the beach?"

"Yes, of course. And lunch at the café in the vineyard?"

"No, not this time. I have another engagement. Is five, at A Cova, OK?"

"Sure," he replied, and Antonio hurried off after giving him a quick hug and words of temporary farewell. Antonio was always hurrying.

He sighed and got up from the table. I think skipping lunch is a sign that I should stop daydreaming about Antonio, he said to himself and paid for the coffees and tapas they had enjoyed. The walk to his car was past historic buildings that always left a sense of wonder in him. Wonder that they had survived so well and wonder that such grand and well-designed structures were there, in such a . . . backwater, was the best way to put it. Monforte de Lemos may have been a major Medieval trading centre, but the medieval days were far behind it. And here in Monforte most of the great buildings were built later, the creations of the seventeenth and eighteenth centuries, and, he assumed, had been largely financed by the gold of the Americas. This, he always thought, was the legacy of that wealth. The magnificent churches and convents.

In the late nineteenth century Monforte had been fortunate to be one of the first Galician cities to get the railway and had flourished again, briefly. Now it was a regional centre that had been contracting for some years while remaining a place where architecture and history were valued.

All in all it was his kind of place, slow paced, safe, clean, scenic, and very friendly. And of course it was far less expensive than Australia, the reason he had washed up here. And also, unexpectedly tolerant. He had expected it in the big cities, Madrid and Barcelona, places he had not visited yet, but here, even in the surrounding small villages, foreigners with a variety of leanings lived undisturbed.

Now he had been here for a while he doubted that Galicia had ever been truly Spanish in the way foreigners thought of Spain historically. Galicia, he felt, was the green jewel that sat atop the Iberian Peninsula, and the Ribeira Sacra, the sacred riverbank, where he now lived, was, in his opinion, the heart of it.

He knew exactly the moment his destiny had been fixed, and who was to blame. It had been Luke. He had been the one to joke that "Spain is cheap" when they, Luke, Bernie, and himself, were sitting in a lakeside cafe north of Sydney, discussing the cost of property in Australia.

He had gone home and checked the Internet and discovered that Spain indeed was far cheaper, and that houses were very, very inexpensive in Green Spain, a region he had never even heard of. His image of Spain had been of a dry, yellow, and flat land, with overbuilt resorts full of foreigners along the coast. He had not envisioned a lush, hilly, green place full of cheap ancient stone houses in

24

picturesque villages overlooking spectacular river valleys full of forests, vineyards, and farmlets. A place with excellent mobile phone coverage and free WiFi in every café, yet one where wild horses, boar, and bear still roamed, along with wolves.

That had been it. He had been hooked. When he found his dream house online, he had not hesitated to put down a deposit. Friends looked at him in horror—buying a house in Spain off the Internet? Mad. But the deposit was only a small amount, and if in a few months he decided the dream was just that, something transient, a passing fancy, he could afford to lose it.

Instead of losing interest, though, he had progressed through all the tedious and stressful steps necessary to make the fantasy a reality. Cleaning up and selling an investment property, getting necessary work done on his own house so it would be ready for renting out. Arranging transport of his furniture, and so forth, and his pets. It was not going to be a short-term move. If he went to Spain it was going to be for at least five years, because of the Australian quarantine laws. He could not afford to take his pets back to Australia.

Of course the dream had been just that, a dream based on a few photos on the Net and very little information. When he had arrived in Spain he was exhausted from a journey of over thirty hours. The next day he had paid up and signed the papers for his house, and then in the afternoon he followed the agent and sellers to it. Well, he would have, if his hire car had not run off the narrow road into a ditch, been damaged, and had to be towed out and away, and he had not had to spend the afternoon getting a replacement hire car. Everyone had been very helpful and concerned, though.

In the dream there had been no thought that the Spanish drove on the wrong side of the road and that after twenty years he would have to relearn to drive a manual car as automatics were rare in Spain. Or that there was a sheer drop on one side of the narrow road to his house that fell 300 metres down a steep rocky slope to a river. The river Mino. It was several days before he saw his house, being driven there by his agent in his Mercedes, but it did not encourage him to try the road again soon. The house itself was not quite as expected. For one thing there was a shower in the entrance hallway, but the house was big and definitely liveable. And the location and views were spectacular. Better than he had dreamed. But the road . . .

He rented a house on a flat road for six months, wondering if with the cheap rents it would be a better long-term proposition, but he was used to living in his own house.

Of course he had got used to narrow winding roads and driving on the wrong side of the road, and eventually used to the road to his house. Though he had been nervous driving on it for a good six months.

And any sense of having made a mistake in coming to Galicia had lasted only the first few days, gone even before he could drive to his house. The people and the place had won him over quickly. It had been the right decision for him and at the right time. A throwaway remark had directed him here and he had no regrets. He wondered though at how such big things in life can hang on a few simple spoken words. Words easily overlooked.

He was almost at his car when his phone rang; and for once he heard it and answered it in time.

"Lunch with you, it is OK," Antonio was saying. "My sister and my mother are taking my aunt to Lugo for lunch and to shop. They know I hate shopping with them, so I do not have to go for lunch. I much prefer to meet you for lunch then a swim in the river. OK?"

"Great," he exclaimed. "We meet at 2:00 p.m.?"

"Of course. I like very much our time together. You do too?"

"Yes, I like very much."

26

"Ah, you are sensitive person and most simpatico. Saturday we meet again."

When he had disconnected, he looked at the phone for a while with a smile on his face and wished he could be as honest and natural in what he said as Antonio was, as the Spanish generally were. And wondered again at how just a few spoken words can make so much difference.

~

La Gorda

*Winner of First Prize, for non-fiction, in "The Good life in Galicia"
short story competition 2016*

La Gorda and the Asociacion Autocaravanistas de Galicia

by J. P. Vincent

A sharp tap on the door of our ancient 1978, twenty-seven-foot-long, American motor home, affectionately known as La Gorda, heralded the arrival of the Asturian Guarda Civil. They very politely asked us to leave the Cudillero harbour car park, where we had been parked up for a couple of days whilst we explored a small part of the Green Coast of Northern Spain. We'd overstayed our welcome.

The two officers with notepads and pens at the ready wandered round our old girl. We were a little concerned and thought we'd committed an offence and they were about to issue a ticket or fine or both. John asked if they were interested in looking inside. Their faces lit up, and, grinning, they stepped up into the old girl. After they had looked under the engine cowling; admired the six-litre non-turboed engine; toured the bathroom, with its shower and hip bath; investigated all the nooks and crannies of the storage systems we'd created whilst renovating her; oh, and after a coffee and a bun, they let us go. Relieved, we drove off slowly, trying not to use too many revs and engulfing the Asturian Guarda in noxious fumes from her exhaust, just in case they changed their minds and did issue those tickets.

Unbeknownst to us, although the local authorities don't mind camper vans and so forth parking overnight in car parks, they only allow you to stay for forty-eight hours. Fair enough.

La Gorda trundled over the Galician border and, with the grace and elegance of a dilapidated barn ravaged by a storm, along the main coastal road, the A8. Mindful that she weighed in at six tons imperial and, if she was four inches wider would have needed a 'convoy exceptional' sticker with support vehicle, we knew many roads and villages were out of bounds to us. That night we ended up parked in front of the hospital in Burela. This was an official camper-van overnight stop, allowing us our forty-eight hours. We parked between two Spanish camper-vans, which looked as if they hadn't moved for several weeks, and settled down for our evening meal. The windows in La Gorda were large, flat, and smoked glass. The owners of the Spanish vans wandered past us several times, peering in and on one occasion jumping up to get a better look. John, my sainted better half and driver of La Gorda because herself, me, was too terrified to drive, opened the door and invited them in for a better look; she was an unusual vehicle after all and a bit of an icon. You don't see many American motor homes in Europe, especially one as old as ours.

After showing them under the engine cowling, the electrical systems, bathroom—you know the drill by now—oh, and a beer this time, as it was far too late for a coffee, they sat at our table and chatted with John. At this time, apart from *hola* and *un café con leche por favor*, I couldn't speak a word of Spanish. John, however, had spent the last fifteen years studying the language in the UK. He was thoroughly enjoying himself and it was possibility the first long conservation he'd had, in Spanish, since crossing the border at Irun, and about a subject that he is also passionate about, vehicles of the classic nature. Me, I did the washing up and listened.

It transpired that the owners of the motor homes that flanked La Gorda were members of the Autocaravanistas de Galicia and were travelling to a reunion in Monforte de Lemos for a Fiesta de Castanas. (Chestnut festival). And would we like to accompany them? The quick and immediate answer was 'yes'. We didn't have a clue where Monforte de Lemos was, or what was there, and had never attended a Galician festival.

Friday arrived and it was confirmed that the organisers were OK with us attending, but our caravanista friends, due to personal circumstances, were unable to come with us. As John had driven across half of Europe, another 120 kilometers wasn't an issue and we decided to go.

We took most of the day to drive the short distance south, firstly because we wanted to enjoy the scenery, which was spectacular, and second because we didn't think we'd be passing this way again, as we were on our way south for the winter. It was November but still mild, T-shirt weather. The hills were green and the villages still retained the last summer flowers and it was warm enough for elderly people to sit on benches outside their houses soaking up the sun.

We arrived in Monforte de Lemos late in the afternoon and drove through the narrow streets of the town looking for our destination, the plaza in front of the Escalapios. It was an impressive building, completely unexpected, grand, and imposing for a small town we'd never heard of.

There were several autocaravanistas already in situ and we were warmly welcomed by the organiser, who waved us into our weekend parking space, right at the front of the plaza. La Gorda, a shabby, old, grubby—we'd been on the road for eighteen months by this time—£500 barn on wheels sat next to sparkling, shiny, thousands of Euros worth of pride and spent pension funds. John did go out and round her to try and clean her up a bit, but a hankie and a bit of spit didn't do much to improve her appearance.

This didn't matter. We were again an icon. We could have made a fortune giving guided tours of 'under the engine cowling etc. etc.'—you already know the rest. Over the weekend, we became part of the wonderful, friendly group of Galicians. We were invited to join them for a Quemada, roast chestnuts, and a disco. Being English, we had an early-to-bed-early-to-rise mentality, and, not used to Spanish hours, we were ready to party by eight p.m. We looked out and there was not a soul in sight, all the other vans were shut up with their curtains drawn. Were we too late or too early? We decided to sit and wait in a nearby bar, and nine p.m. then ten p.m. passed and still no sign of anyone. Ten thirty and the first van door opened and party-goers began to emerge. It was nearly time for our bed.

But we persisted, joined in with all the activities, except that the plants near our table were given an extra drink of Aguadiente or two, and we had a wonderful time. The following day, or should I say, later the same day, as we'd gone to bed at five a.m., we were taken on a coach trip to the railway museum, another of John's loves; up to the Parador hotel, which was once a monastery; and on a tour of the Escalapios. During the afternoon we went on a little journey of exploration of our own and visited the Tourist Information Office, where we met a very knowledgeable lady, who, I might add, is still a very good friend of ours, who gave us an insight into Monforte and the surrounding area.

Monday morning arrived and the members of the Autocaravanistas de Galicia packed up and trundled off to their respective homes. We decided we'd like to stay a little longer and explore the area, and we found the 'Aire' or official overnight stop for camper-vans, behind the multi-usos building, which houses the music, singing and dance studios. The Aire had beautiful views of the magnificent Parador, Tower of Homage, and the church of San Vicente of the Pines, and beside us ran the river Cabe. The sun was still shining and our lady from the Tourist Information Office came and took us on a tour of the magnificent Canyons de Sil, the vineyards that have been producing wine since Roman times, and a taster history lesson of the area and its people.

We arrived in Galicia by default, or by the design of a higher power, depending on your view, for a weekend of celebrating with a group of friendly, helpful, and sociable Galician people. And four and a half years later we are still here celebrating with friendly, helpful, and sociable Galician people who have drawn us into a lifestyle that we found suits us.

Our lives have been changed by Galicia, its people, and its history beyond anything that I can understand, or its magic has allowed us to find our true selves. Our travelling days aren't over, because we have family in other parts of the world, but we always come home to Galicia.

~

Jesus Speaks Galician

by Olivia Stowe

So that's why she didn't come to the funeral—didn't even acknowledge my letter—Penny thought. She put her forehead to the cold glass in the window overlooking the village street, gazing with a detached vision at the blanket of early December snow, which was covering the street and narrow front garden with a lovely covering of white. But Penny wasn't fooled. She knew the ugliness and neglect that was hidden below the snow. She knew this would be a bleak Christmas for her, like so many of the others she had gritted her teeth through over the years while others basked in the glow of the season within the bosoms of their families. She let her shoulders sag and loosened her finger hold on the typed letter, letting it flutter to the floor.

She had thought that it was because Millie still carried the resentment of their parents—their father an ever-complaining tyrant and their mother a whiny alcoholic. The estrangement had sent Millie spinning out of England to Spain, where she'd been this last decade and more, answering Penny's letters with only terse responses—not answering their father's few, complaining and judgmental letters at all. Not that Penny would have answered the letters from her father to Millie that she'd gotten a glimpse of either—full of bitterness and judgment for Millie having gone off with a foreigner and not, to anyone's knowledge, having ever married him.

35

Penny knew why Millie hadn't married Rodrigo. He already was married, and, being Catholic, there would be no divorce even if there was no love. He'd been older than Millie. Millie had let Penny know when Rodrigo had died, but her father had been so bitter about it that neither one had bothered to tell him.

Now this letter—from a hospital in Lugo, Spain, from some sort of patient representative, a sister someone or other. Penny's father buried not more than a week and Penny, who had taken full care of him at his village house during his last two months, only now beginning to wrap up his affairs and go back to her job in the book store. It was the Christmas season. The bookstore would need all of its employees pulling overtime. They hadn't been kind about holding her job for her while she cared for her father in his last days—certainly not considering how much time and effort she'd given them for over a decade. The bookstore was her total life now, but it didn't seem like she meant that much to the bookstore.

The problem was that now the hospital in Spain wanted to send Millie back to her house. There wasn't anything they could do for her; the cancer was too far advanced. She was insisting on going home to die. But there had to be someone there to receive Millie and take care of her. Penny was the only relative of hers that Millie had identified on her admittance forms, and she claimed there was no one in Spain to take care of her. Penny knew, though, that her job wouldn't be held for her to allow her to attend another relative through a terminal illness—certainly not during the Christmas season.

With a sigh, Penny reached down and picked the letter up off the floor. Family was family, no matter how estranged. She sank down into the chair at the old secretary, read the address at the top of the letter and the sister's name, and began to write her return letter.

* * * *

Penny hadn't expected to be met by anyone at the airport in Santiago. She'd sent her flight number and arrival time in the letter telling Sister Noela at the Lugo hospital she was coming, but she hadn't received an answer. But there was a younger man—at least young in Penny's mind, as she was a bit past thirty herself—standing in the reception hall, waving a sign with her name on it. How many Penelope Stanleys could there be coming off the same flight in northwestern Spain?

"Senora Stanley?" he asked rather hesitatingly when she came and stood in front of him and pointed to his sign. She had never thought of herself as tall, but she was a couple of inches taller than he was. Other than that he seemed normal and was supporting an engaging smile. He was dark haired and a bit swarthy but quite presentable. Looking at him now, she could see that he probably was older than she was, maybe even ten years. If so, the years had treated him well.

"Yes, I am Penny Stanley," she answered, trying to give him a smile that equaled his, but she'd just come off a long day catching her flight without knowing where she was going from here other than the address of her sister's house somewhere in the region, somewhere on a mountain slope above the Minho River, if she remembered rightly what her sister had once written to her. She had no idea how far it was from the Santiago airport, though. She could tell from the map that there was a good distance between Santiago and Lugo, where the hospital was.

"I am Xesús," the man said in halting and heavily accented, but easily understood, English. "Xesús has come to take you to your home. I know you didn't expect anyone from the family to meet you—the hospital didn't know that your sister had family here until it was too late to inform you." Penny was quick to adjust to the man's way of referring to himself by name, although it made her smile each time she heard it. She also was greatly relieved to

37

know that there was someone here with connections to Millie, and that she didn't have to figure out everything for herself.

My home? Penny thought. Hardly, although she couldn't say where her home was at the moment. Her own flat in Reading was just a rental and she'd put her father's house close to Oxford up for sale—and already had offers on that, as housing was tight in the university town. It had also been uplifting to discover that houses, even a modest one like her father had lived in, went for a good price in the Oxford area. If she could find a far cheaper economy to live in, she could squeak by on the interest from what she'd get for the house without having to continue working herself. As she was afraid, the bookstore had let her go, and she didn't have a specific job to go back to. She wasn't that fond of her flat in Reading, either, so "home" was something to be negotiated at this point when the time came. It certainly wasn't in a remote area of hot and dusty Spain, though.

"Did you say Jesus? Is your name really Jesus?" she asked, trying, unsuccessfully to keep the tone of disbelief and challenge out of her voice. That couldn't be right.

He just beamed back at her. "Yes. We don't spell it as you would, but it's the same name. We use that name in Spain. Spanish Catholics believe in instilling the attributes of the Holy Family in our families. My father's name was Xesús and his father's name was Xesús. So, my name is Xesús. My brother is Joseph and my mother is Maria. So . . ."

"Oh, well, that's interesting," Penny said. And strange, she thought, but she didn't want to start off on the wrong foot with anyone here—especially someone who had met her at the airport to take her to Millie's house.

As they drove east from Santiago, she appreciated even more that someone had come to pick her up, as the journey was long and the route convoluted. But she also was surprised to find that her impression of Spain as hot and dusty didn't hold for this Galician region. The hills were rolling and still lush with vegetation. It was been a crazy year in weather across Europe, and winter had not reached northern Spain yet. It was as green as England was in summer—even more green if that was possible—while being wilder and more lush in foliage and with steeper slopes running down to the faster-flowing waterways. The villages they passed on the way were even smaller and less-ordered than those in the Reading area and as old, if not older, most being made out of stone, many unoccupied and falling down—but in a picturesque way.

She wouldn't have known that Christmas was approaching if many of the houses didn't already have colored lights and a smattering of outdoor Christmas ornaments on display.

It was nearly dark when they arrived at a hodge-podge of stone cottages set at angles and closely abutting a small, winding road high above a meandering river, with a checkerboard of garden plots, many planted to grapevines, tumbling down the slope to the water. Nothing was in flower or full leaf now, of course, but it didn't take much to envision how vital this countryside would look in full bloom.

"Fincas," Xesús explained as he maneuvered along a road hugging the side of the mountain and observed Penny looking down at the pattern of small plots.

"Fincas?"

"Yes, through the centuries family holdings of the fields became divided and subdivided and families intermarried to the point that everything is divided into small plots—fincas—and a family now could have a series of the plots located separately so that they have to do more walking than tending of the plots to cover them all in a day. Senora de Peres has several of the fincas down there."

"Senora de Peres?"

"Yes, your sister." Xesús gave her a quizzical look.

"Ah, yes," Penny said. So, Millie was going by the name Peres here rather than Stanley. That must have been Rodrigo's surname. They will think the two of them were married here; it's likely they didn't know Rodrigo had a wife elsewhere. That was natural enough, she supposed. If the villagers knew of their living arrangements, they likely would be unwelcoming, and Millie wasn't one to take an effort to make friends herself.

Xesús pulled up in front of a stone cottage that looked like a ruin and that was so close to the road that the small Fiat Xesús was driving barely had room to park between the road and the rock wall. A door opened, and light spilled out onto the Fiat before it was stifled by the figure of a heavyset, elderly woman.

"Dores. From the village. She has been sitting with Senora de Peres," Xesús explained.

And so it began. Millie had already been sent home from the hospital to die. Yet another ordeal of vigilance to the end for Penny—her last living relative, and yet another one who she had not been close to in life. She hauled herself out of the Fiat and reached for her suitcase, but Xesús was faster than she was at hefting it. The village woman, Dores, gave her a stiff, "Hola. Buenas," and an "it's about time you got here" look as she stood aside for Penny to enter the cottage.

The two women had barely acknowledged each other at the door before Dores had turned to return to the sick room and Penny's attention had been arrested by seeing a decorated Christmas tree beside a fireplace in which a fire had been laid. She almost cried. She hadn't had time to even think about decorating a tree before she'd left England.

Seeing where her gaze was turned, Xesús gently said, "Christmas trees are important back in England. We thought—"

"Yes, yes, thank you, Xesús. It's lovely." And indeed it was. Already the heaviness that had been weighing her

40

down for what it seemed like years was lifting. "Now, maybe I should see my sister," she said, pulling herself back into reality.

* * * *

Millie had settled down at last, the effects of the morphine finally having taken hold. Penny had held and rocked her just as she'd seen the village woman, Dores, doing while Xesús was showing her around the cottage. There hadn't been much to see inside the house, and it was a work in progress, although the "progress" part of the work was well done. There was the main room that served as living room, dining room, and kitchen. This room, as well as Millie's, off to the left as the cottage was entered, had been tastefully renovated with some sections of the wall being stone and some white plasterboard. The plasterboard sections were hung with abstract landscapes that obviously were from the village area and were masterfully done. Lights hung over these, the only lighting in the room other than the glowing Christmas tree, to which Penny's eyes frequently wandered in appreciation. Millie's bedroom was large, with a similar wall treatment. A modernized bath and large walk-in closet were on the street side of this wing, and the bedroom opened up onto a stone terrace that ran the full length of the house on the back, with a view down the slope to the Minho River and up the mountainside on the other side of the narrow river valley.

The room to which Xesús had taken Penny's suitcase was on the other side of the house. Her bedroom was small, but also opened out onto the terrace in back. The walls were just stone and the room obviously hadn't been renovated yet. A primitive bath, entered from both sides, separated it from a room, also not renovated, on the front of the house, which obviously was an office and catchall room. From the art supplies strewn about, it also had once been used as an art studio. The unfinished

41

paintings were by the same hand as those on the walls in the renovated part of the house. Rodrigo? Penny wondered. She couldn't think of Millie as having artistic talent. But she was having difficulty remembering anything about Millie, who was nearly ten years Penny's senior and had left England and, as she put it, "the clutches of her family," when Penny was too young and alienated from the family herself to pay much attention.

She didn't know any more about Rodrigo—other than that Millie said, when she'd left, that she'd follow him to the ends of the earth if she had too. As Penny remembered it, her father's major objection—her mother was too deep into the bottle to voice much of an opinion one way or other—was that Rodrigo had been a good ten years older than Millie was—and was a foreigner and a dreamer.

Being a dreamer obviously was a sin in Penny's parents' eyes.

Dores, in a language Penny couldn't fathom and that didn't seem like Spanish, which Penny had some familiarity with, attempted to convey Millie's pain killer injection schedule to Penny. Xesús, who said Dores was speaking Galician—more like Portuguese than Spanish—interpreted as best he could. Penny managed to get across that she knew all about applying the drugs, as she had just been through that with her father and only needed to know the schedule. When that had been dispensed with, she suddenly found herself alone.

All alone, sitting beside a lowly moaning woman who was a mere bag of bones version of the sister she had known so little and so long ago. All alone in a stone cottage, perched on a mountainside who knew where. All alone. Penny had to make frequent trips out to the living room to look at the Christmas tree to keep from sinking into depression.

When Millie's breathing became regular, Penny rose from beside the bed and started to wander more purposely around the small house. The light was dim in the main room other than around the Christmas tree. She went to the refrigerator, which was almost bare. What would they do for food, she wondered. Where could she get some? How could she get some? There was a jug in the refrigerator and she quickly ascertained that it had wine in it. She found a wine glass—there didn't seem to be any dearth of wine glasses in the kitchen. Millie quite likely was her mother's daughter. But Penny wouldn't be catty about that at this moment. She couldn't think of anything more that she wanted—no, needed—at this moment, than wine.

She poured herself a glass, pulled a throw blanket off the back of a sofa to wrap around herself, wandered out onto the terrace, and sat in a patio chair there. The moon was full and picked out the checkerboard pattern of fields—what Xesús had said were fincas—cascading like folds in a blanket down to the ribbon of water below, reflecting the light of the moon. She sighed. The view was divine. The wine was delicious. After a few minutes, though, she shook her head. She wasn't anywhere close to be in the mood to be seduced by this wild and primitive country. She was still in the mood to feel sorry for herself and at a loss of how she could be expected to carry on here.

She rose and walked back into the house, letting her feet carry her to what had been the studio at the front of the house, with its intriguing mysteries. It wasn't just the stacks of paintings, many unfinished, to explore. When Xesús had breezed her through the room before, she'd seen that there was an old secretary desk there with papers strewn across the top. She'd even seen the envelope with her name on it propped up on the base of the desk lamp.

She sat at the desk and fingered the envelope. She returned it to its resting place and took a swig of her wine. She wasn't ready to face whatever that said yet. Her eye went to a couple of folded pages that looked like documents. The thicker of the two seemed to be a will. Ah, good, progress, she thought. Whether there was one and where it could be found had been a worry in the back of her mind all the time she was flying here. She had no idea what, if anything, Millie had to leave behind—let alone who she'd leave it to. She only knew that she'd be left doing something about it. She had kept forcing those worries into the background as being ghoulish to be thinking about yet.

She folded the official-looking document open now. It was in Spanish and hard to decipher, but she saw Millie's name—with the surname "Peres"—and her own on the first sheet. There were three sheets of paper, the other two with Millie's name but someone else's—a different name on each sheet. There were lists of bequests—probably of property—under the names on each sheet. The light was too dim to make it all out, but the listings weren't identical. They seemed to be for different property.

Just then, the other legal-looking document was disturbed and fell open. This too was in Spanish, but this was more identifiable. It was a marriage certificate. The names on it were Rodrigo Peres Varela and Millicent Stanley de Peres. It was dated some six years earlier. So, they *were* married. But Millie had never thought to notify either their father or Penny. Why would Millie keep this from Penny? Millie had communicated rarely and then only tersely, but Penny had regularly . . . but then, no, she hadn't. She'd followed Millie's lead more than eight years ago. She'd stopped writing too because little was coming back. And that was before the marriage. Still . . .

Penny reached back for the will to more closely examine that, but just then the lights went out.

Her first thought was what sort of backwater place was this that cut the power at night. That was her second thought too, but then she thought, oh, well, she was exhausted anyway and had experienced too much today already. She downed the last of the wine in her glass and felt her way through the connecting bathroom to what would be her bedroom, just barely tolerable in its unrenovated condition.

Groping around, she found that there was a candle in a holder on her bed stand, with matches beside it. She took this as further evidence that the power was routinely cut at night in the village. The candle gave her enough light to pull nightclothes out of her suitcase, use the primitive bathroom facilities, and climb into bed.

She was awakened sometime after dawn by the cries of pain coming from across the house. Damn, she thought, looking at her clock and springing out of bed. She'd missed the injection schedule by an hour. Her first testing with taking care of her sister, and she'd bungled the time by an hour. Millie must be in deep pain.

Injecting the morphine and getting under Millie and rocking her body until the cries and sobbing subsided took longer than Penny had imagined it would. Dores had been so good about it the previous night and Penny was so clumsy. Penny would give anything to have the old village woman here now, and she was sure that Millie thought the same, to the extent that Millie could think anything.

Millie was lucid, though, for a brief moment or two between the pain killer deadening the pain took effect and put her into a merciful painless dreamland. It was just a moment of recognition. Her eyes turned to Penny and a voice Penny recognized across the years weakly said, "Penny? You've come?"

Penny castigated herself later for her response, automatic, unthinking. "You were married, Millie. You didn't tell us."

Millie's eyes went dull, she muttered, "You wouldn't have cared if I did," and she turned her face to the wall and was unconscious.

Sitting there on the side of the bed, the frail body of her older sister still in her embrace, Penny began to cry silently. She rocked her sister's inert body back and forth, murmuring over and over again, "I would have cared. I would have cared." Getting control of herself, she worked her way from underneath Millie and arranged her sister as comfortably as she could be in the bed.

Standing, she looked down at Millie as she smoothed down the flanks of her nightdress. "Oh, Millie, Millie, Millie. What has become of our family?" she murmured.

Not that there would be a family for her for very much longer. She already felt the loneliness slicing through her.

* * * *

A couple of hours later, Penny groped her way into the main room and over to the kitchen area, set up by an island counter. She stared, with regret, at the collapsed, obviously empty, coffee packet and electric coffeepot, unusable with the power still being off. She barely had time to open the unpowered refrigerator to scout out if there was anything that resembled breakfast for her that hadn't spoiled, when there was a knock at the door. When she opened it, Xesús breezed past her with a cardboard box filled with groceries. She caught up with him in time to retrieve the package of ground coffee from on top.

"Xesús forgot to tell you where the nearest market was," he said. "So Xesús got a few things for you."

"Would it help to know where the grocery store is?" Penny asked. "How would I get there?" She recognized that she sounded a bit petulant. She couldn't help it. Everyone else blamed morning grouch on the lack of coffee; she do so with the best of them. Was she the only one to realize how marooned and out of her element she was here?

"There's the Renault. You can drive when you've found the way."

"The Renault?"

"Yes, under the terrace. The garage. Do you know how to drive?"

"Yes. Of course."

46

"The refrigerator isn't working," he said, the door open, the light inside not on.

"No, the power hasn't come back on," Penny said.

"Come back on? How did it go off?"

"You don't lose power at night in the village? It's been off since last night."

"No, we don't lose power at night. Do you have your power cut at night in England?"

"No, of course not."

"We don't either. Here. Xesús will be back soon." He handed her the half-unloaded box and disappeared through the front door. Penny barely had time to unload the rest of the groceries before he was back with a short, grizzled-looking, middle-aged man. The lights had already come back on right before the two men showed up.

"Bad fuse," Xesús explained. "Viter fixed. This is Viter." Penny and the Spaniard acknowledged each other, while Xesús continued. "Viter lives two houses down. He did the work on this house. He can finish for you, if you want. You have any trouble like power going out, just go get Viter. Viter is Xesús' father's cousin."

"Are you all related in this village?" Penny asked, as a joke.

"Mostly, yes," Xesús answered seriously.

At that moment there was another knock at the door. When she opened the door, she could have hugged Dores and pulled her inside. As far as Penny knew Dores had been finished here last night and Penny was entirely on her own now. It only took the one time having to medicate Millie for Penny to know how ill prepared she was to take over totally. Millie was a much more difficult patient than Penny's father had been—and so frail that Penny was afraid she'd break each time Penny touched her.

Penny didn't hug the woman, though, not only because Dores was still taking on a stern countenance, but also because the old woman was holding a basket in front of her. Behind her was another woman, thinner and taller

47

than Dores, but still elderly. She held a large oblong loaf of bread.

Handing Penny the basket, Dores marched past her and straight to the bedroom, where, on cue, Millie was rousing and beginning to moan in pain. The other woman stopped in front of Penny, smiled shyly, perched the loaf of bread on top of the contents of the basket, and then continued on past to the kitchen counter.

"Maria," Xesús explained to Penny. "She'll help tidy up the house." And, after another shy bob, Maria started doing just that, giving the door into Millie's bedroom a wide berth.

"Now, Xesús will be back this afternoon to show you where your fincas are. Wear something you can work in a garden in. The weather has been strange this year. Whereas you were getting winter in England, winter hasn't appeared here yet this year. We haven't had a frost yet and the weeds know that."

"But I'll have my sister to take care of."

"This is not a sprint, Senora Stanley. Dores will go soon, but she'll be back after lunch to watch Senora de Peres for a few hours. You need to have breaks."

"Dores will come back?"

"Yes, as long as she is needed and you need breaks. We are all family here. We will do this together."

Penny stood at the door, almost in tears, as she waved Xesús and Viter down the narrow street toward where Viter's house must be located.

* * * *

"You are a good worker," Xesús said, as they arrived back at the Fiat parked at the end of a row of grape vine frames and he brought out a bottle of wine. "You work fast and don't complain."

"When you told me we would be weeding in the vineyard and garden finca, I thought the job would be too big to tackle," Penny said, as she collapsed against the car and gratefully received a glass of wine. "My sister must have been in the hospital for some time and not have been able to tend to the fields for quite some time before that."

"The whole village took on the work," Xesús answered.

"Ah, that part about you being one big family."

"Yes."

"Tell me—I haven't really seen my sister for a long time—did she get along well in the village?"

"You sister was . . . she was a difficult woman to get along with."

"Ah, I'm not surprised. But the village is treating her like family anyway? I've seen how good and patient Dores is with her, even though I don't discern any affection for Millie there. Is it her sense of treating everyone in the village as family?"

"Yes, of course, why not—because she *is* family."

"I don't understand."

"Dores Varela is Rodrigo's mother. She did her duty correctly to your sister as Rodrigo's wife, and she is helping to care for your sister because she is family. She could not hold her head up in the village if she didn't do what she could for family. Dores does it for Rodrigo, though, not for your sister. It is complicated. It was clear that Rodrigo loved your sister and that she loved him. But . . ."

"But what, Xesús?"

"But Maria is Dores' best friend in the world, and her cousin, so she has always been reserved with your sister."

"Maria? The woman who came with Dores this morning to clean? I noticed that she didn't come close to my sister's bedroom. Did she and my sister not get along?"

"At some distance. They were family too, but—"

Penny laughed. "This family business seems quite incestuous. How is Maria family to Millie?"

"Rodrigo's first wife, Antía, was Maria's daughter. But once she had died and Rodrigo married your sister, even though they had been living together for some time already, your sister became family too. There is no choice in who is family and who isn't." He looked like he thought Penny was going to dispute that assertion and that he'd have to repeat it more forcefully. Penny didn't challenge him, though. As Millie's sister, she realized she had to respond to any of this family business gently and with sensitivity.

"And you, where do you fit into this family, Xesús?" she asked, assuming she had reached the end of this string at last, flabbergasted at how interrelated the villagers were—and that Millie could become—and couldn't escape—being accepted into their family simply by marrying Rodrigo.

"Maria is my mother; Antía was my sister."

The conversation paused there as Penny tried to catch her breath at this revelation. This man, who had been so kind and supportive of her was the brother of the woman Penny's sister had wronged for so many years. Penny was breathless at the mind-set of the strength of family and of the simple goodness of these Galician people.

"I'm so sorry, Xesús. I didn't realize. You can't have liked my sister very much—and you can't have wanted to help me very much either, as I am her sister."

"As I said, your sister is a difficult woman," Xesús said, but then he smiled. "I don't find you a difficult woman, though, at all, and I would help you even if I did, because . . ."

"Because I'm family," Penny finished for him, and they both laughed, clinked glasses, and took a long drag on their wine. "I must say you people extend the concept of family quite a bit. Let's see, I'm the sister to Rodrigo's second wife and you are the brother of his first, the relationship of all of us to Rodrigo makes you and me family."

50

"If you think about it, all of us on earth are family," Xesús answered, "and wouldn't it be well if we all thought in those terms?"

There wasn't anything Penny could say to that. She just smiled, comforted by the thought and wishing that it could be so.

Later that night, after she had managed to settle Millie down, Penny went back to the secretary in the studio and picked up the will again. This time, under stronger light of the candle in addition to the desk lamp, she looked more closely at the three separate bequests that had been made. The first set, this house, the fincas Xesús had taken her to today, the Renault under the terrace, and the surrender value of Millie's annuity from her job as a writer were being left to her. A house in the village, presumably Rodrigo's family home, a few parcels of land, and half of the liquid assets went to a Dores Varela. Rodrigo's mother. Dores also was to receive Rodrigo's paintings, with the exception of a small one, a portrait of Millie showing a rare smile and now hanging in Millie's bedroom. This painting was to be buried with Millie along with photographs of Rodrigo. The third bequest, yet another village house, parcels of land, and half of the liquid assets went to a Maria Cela. The mother of Rodrigo's first wife and sister of Xesús.

Then, and only then, did Penny reach for the envelope with her name on it that she hadn't opened the previous night when the power went out. The letter, as well as the envelope, was addressed to her. She read the short note.

I at last am facing the reality of going to the hospital with this cancer and chances are good I won't be coming out again. There isn't much to say to you now other than I'm sorry we are apart and I wish you well, Penny.

I am leaving you a small house in a village that has become both hell and paradise to me. I hope that the bequest will be enough to draw you here and give you the family that neither of us were provided in England. It was tough going for me here, especially after I lost

Rodrigo. I brought it on myself, but Rodrigo was worth every moment of it. I hope you can find the inner joy I have from this slice of paradise and a man as good as my Rodrigo. There is a family here for you if you want one. These people never give up. I'm sure they will be surprised as hell, though, that I'm giving most of Rodrigo back to them. I only hope that I am giving you to them as well—and them to you. If you stay, please try to be a better family member than I was. I wish I at least was a better sister than I was and brought you away with me in the first place. I know you will find this hard to believe, but I would have come to Father's funeral if I could have. It would have been for you—and me—though, not for him.

* * * *

Millie's note had touched Penny. Not that it didn't have the same hurt and bitter flare of the woman Penny had known in previous written exchanges with her—their actual face-to-face time was too buried in the past and in family conflict for Penny to remember it. It was, rather, the recognition in the note that family could have beneficial power and that, in the end, Millie was giving back to her Galician family and showing them some, albeit begrudged, appreciation.

This knowledge made it easier for Penny to care for Millie, who was drifting off but too stubborn to give up yet. Penny found that she could hold Millie more tenderly and competently through the rough periods, which were decreasing in frequency and intensity as Millie's body lost strength and she floated ever further away from the present world. Millie didn't fight her when Penny cleansed her with a wet washcloth and there was less whimpering in Millie's unconsciousness. Millie hadn't uttered another word to Penny, though, since that first one about not caring, and there was no recognition given that Penny was even there.

In the same circumstances, Penny had resented the bitter, almost judgmental, response from her father as he was dying. But now, with Millie, because of the note and

Millie's reverting of her husband's property to his family—other than the property given to Penny with the stated purpose that Penny could, at last, find family herself—Penny could let all of the resentment and hurt feelings evaporate. She was better prepared now just make her sister's last days as comfortable for her and loving for both of them as possible.

Each day Dores and Maria appeared in the afternoon to relieve Penny for a couple of hours. Penny came to see Dores' stiffness as just her way and Dores was nothing but kind toward both Penny and her sister. With each visit, Penny was picking up another Galician word to use in communication with Dores and Dores was managing an added English word herself. It wasn't lost on Penny that in all the years Millie was with Rodrigo, Dores must have resisted learning any English to aid communication with Millie and yet she was making an effort to meet Penny halfway.

Maria frequently attended with Dores and puttered around the house, cleaning what hadn't gotten dirty, and giving Penny shy, but friendly looks—but not going near the room where Millie was drifting away. This also wasn't lost on Penny—that Maria had such strong ties with Dores that she wouldn't let her friend handle this alone and that she openly accepted Penny even though Penny was the sister to the woman who had snatched the husband of Maria's daughter away from her.

Xesús appeared daily, too, always with some new way to pull Penny's mind and body away from caring for her sister, if only for an hour or two. Thus it was that he appeared early Friday evening, with Dores and Maria in tow, and declared that Penny was going with him into the nearest town of any size, Monforte de Lemos, to join in a regular meeting of English-speaking residents of the region for cultural pursuits in that language.

"Or, rather, you'll be taking Xesús," he said. "We'll take the Renault. You'll drive. So, this is really to get you used to driving the car here. Although it will be good for you to meet with others who wish to exercise their English."

"Is that why your English is so good?" Penny asked, with a chuckle. "Because you meet with this group."

"But, of course. You do not think Xesús' English is excellent?"

"Yes, it certainly is," Penny responded—especially the quaint way of substituting your name for "I" much of the time, she thought.

The English speakers, not many more than a dozen of them beyond Penny and Xesús, met inside a café in Monforte de Lemos, while, thanks to the unseasonably warm spell, the outdoor tables were still active and a guitarist was entertaining out there. The café was decorated for Christmas both inside and outside, and a portable heater warmed those outside, Galicians were fighting the march into the coldness of winter for as long as they could. Penny found the muffled sound of the Spanish guitar to be a mellowing influence on the buzz of English being spoken in the room, and she couldn't remain untouched by the decorations of the season. Those present constituted an almost equal proportion of Galicians honing their language skills and foreigners who already spoke English.

She was especially smitten with a handsome man with a wavy mane of salt-and-pepper-hued hair who appeared to be in his mid forties and who stood tall and straight and confident, commanding the room as he positioned himself by the fire and a Christmas tree. People were being drawn to him to bask in his smile and easy laughter, as he naturally became the focus of attention without consciously monopolizing attention.

"Would you like to meet him?" Xesús said, leaning over to whisper in Penny's ear.

"Who? Oh, the man over there with the books under his arm?"

"Yes. That's Paulo, the one giving the readings this evening."

Before Penny could say whether or not she wanted to meet him, Xesús had dragged her over to Paulo and was introducing her. The man turned a winning and interested smile on Penny, and she, like everyone else in the room had done, melted to him.

"So, you have come to hear love poetry?" he asked. His voice was a rich baritone. He went on before she could answer, "I'm glad cousin Xesús has brought new, and oh so lovely, blood into the group. We are usually quite sparse on poetry evening."

"Poetry?" Penny asked, blushing because he had taken one of her hands in his and she could feel a tingling sensation running up her arm.

"Yes," he said, taking the books from under his arm and holding them up. "First our own Galician romance poet, Roselíta de Castro, from her *Cantares gallegos*. And then because Roselíta can be so melancholy and because this is an English-speaking group, from Elizabeth Barrett Browning's *Sonnets from the Portuguese*. So much more hopeful, don't you think? I'll read them both in Galician and English versions. I love the sound of the Galician language, but I don't want the English speakers to miss the power of the words. Roselíta was the first one who wrote in our regional language, you know, and she was heavily criticized in Madrid for doing so. But now she's recognized as a national treasure. I hope you will love the sound of the poetry in Galician as well."

"Yes, of course," Penny murmured, having no idea who De Castro was, but not wanting to disagree with anything this fabulous man beside her said. Then she laughed, and, eyes twinkling, Paulo laughed too, before a women put a hand on his shoulder, saying she wanted to show him something about the lectern from which he'd be reading. Penny hadn't laughed about poetry, though, but because it had just hit her that Xesús had said he was a cousin. Yet more family.

"Who is that fascinating man?" Penny asked Xesús as Paulo moved away from them. "You said he was a cousin."

"That's Paulo Peres Varela, Rodrigo's younger brother. He teaches English literature at the University of Santiago de Compostela."

"Rodrigo's brother?" Penny asked. "And is he as good as Rodrigo was?"

Xesús laughed. "They were both very good men, Penny. But in different ways. Rodrigo was the better painter and Paulo the better poet. But, as men, both good—very good, yes. Very good family."

Xesús, of course, didn't realize what Penny was really referring too, and only now, causing her to laugh a happy, tinkling laugh again, did Penny herself realize why she'd asked that question. She remembered now the sentence in Millie's letter hoping that Penny could find as good a man here as Rodrigo had been.

"Is he married?" she blurted out.

Xesús laughed again. "Only to his poetry at this point. But he is a widower and it's high time he found another worthy wife." Penny turned to look into Xesús' face to see that he was giving her a sharp look—amusement with something else in it, as well. Hope perhaps? Perhaps this outing to meet with other English speakers wasn't as random a choice of Xesús' as she'd assumed.

She blushed and decided she needed to change the subject—not that she really was changing the subject. "You said that Viter is the one who renovated the modern part of Millie's house. Do you think he'd be interested in renovating the other part too?"

"I'm sure he would. Are you thinking of getting a better price for it fully renovated?"

"I'm thinking of living there myself," Penny said, the answer surprising her as much as it obviously pleased Xesús.

"Good," he said and just then a waiter came up to them to get their drink orders. The waiter didn't seem to understand Penny's question of whether they had a favorite brand of local white wine. Xesús interjected with a "I don't think he understands English. I'll ask him. Xesús speaks Galician."

Jesus certainly does speak Galician, Penny thought, truly happy and content for the first time in years. She only now realized how long her elusive search for a family had been and that she had found one for herself in Galicia—if she didn't screw this up. Or, rather, perhaps, Millie had given her a family as a last, parting gift—with an assist now from Xesús. She wasn't alone.

If any people on earth understood what it meant to be Jesus' people, she thought, it had to be the Galicians.

~

Vines growing on the Río Miño

Vendimia in the Ribeira Sacra in Galicia

by Stephen Bush

From January to October life in the Ribeira Sacra region of Galicia revolves around its vineyards and the grapes they are to produce. And Vendimia, the grape harvest, is the frenzy of picking and crushing, followed by the eating and drinking and fiestas (parties) in the afternoons, which end each year's season of the grapes. Vendimia starts when the grapes are ready to be picked, and the starting date can vary by over a month from year to year. In the last ten years it has started as early as late August and as late as the second of October.

Many hundreds of villages and a dozen small towns lie within the river valleys of the Sil and Miño rivers that compose what is known as the Ribeira Sacra, and their vineyards are of great importance to every community. Most grapes are still grown on small plots of land. A family may have one vineyard plot or many vineyards scattered around a village or town. The distribution of land belonging to a family is the result of inheritances and marriages over the centuries, and the modern result is a region filled with a picturesque patchwork of vineyards and vegetable gardens (huertas), as well as many untended plots of land that are returning to the forest, which link the small villages and towns, each with its own collection of ancient stone houses.

In recent years there has been some amalgamation of the small vinyas into large vineyards and major winemakers have emerged, but they still account for only a small part of the grapes harvested and wine made.

Vines in the Ribeira Sacra are mostly of the red Mencia variety, with the white Godello being the most common white wine grape grown. Other varieties are far less important. All vines receive a lot of personal care throughout the period from January to October, with pruning, clearing, spraying, and more clearing and spraying occurring as the season progresses, right up to two or three weeks before the grapes are harvested. All this work is done by hand, and for many vineyard owners it is important that the pruning and care of the vines is done in tune with the cycles of the moon. The narrow roads that wind into the river valleys become extra busy on what are believed to be the auspicious days. The vineyard workers, usually the owners or a relative, park where they can on the narrow and often steep roads. Once they have found a parking place, they often have some distance still to go and climb the rocky paths, which usually are only wide enough for one person to walk them at a time, to their vineyards.

Small vinyard on the bank of the River Sil

Most Ribeira Sacra vines are grown on rock-walled terraces hand built over the centuries. These terraces climb the steep sides of the canyons of the Sil, in places up to a 600 meters deep, and the Miño, nearly 400 meters deep. Many small plots are only reachable on foot and there are a few vineyards in the canyon of the river Sil that can only be reached by boat.

The rivers Sil and Miño were dammed in the 1960s to provide hydroelectric power. Before that the canyons fell to an even greater depth. Many villages and vineyards were lost when the valleys were flooded. The depth and shape of the winding river canyons create numerous micro climates that are warmer and wetter than the surrounding, higher, land, and this is one of the secrets of the Riberia Sacra as a wine-growing region. Another secret is that, though the region is full of rock, the soil on the river banks is rich—thick, damp, alluvial soil full of organic matter and nutrients that, over the millenniums, has washed down from the surrounding hills, hills that are nearly all still covered in natural pine forest and patches of Spanish Oak, not depleted farmland, so the soils of the valley vineyards are replenished constantly.

Looking at the valley walls, the pattern of still-cultivated vineyards, seems haphazard till you learn that those that face north get less sun and colder winds and produce fewer grapes and those that face south get more sun and the warm winds and produce more. Many productive vineyards have fallen out of cultivation as the growers have concentrated on the best-yielding plots.

On the terraces the season's work normally begins in January with pruning. It is midwinter and the mornings in the valleys are misty and cold. There may even be frosts and occasional snowfalls on the hills. Few vineyards are accessible by machinery that is not carried on the back of a man, and pruning a vineyard may take a man a few hours if it is small or several men a few days if it is large. Experience will tell the pruner how each branch on each vine must be cut to ensure the most grapes and the best harvest for the coming season.

Vines on the Banks of the Mino

The Ribeira Sacra is one of several recognised Denominations of Origin in Galicia. It became an official Denomintión de Origen in 1997, but the area has been home to vineyards since it was under Roman rule. These Denominations are similar to the Appelations of France, and in accredited vineyards the care of the vines is closely monitored not only by the vineyard owner but also by the Denomination body. Not all vineyards in the region are accredited. It is a choice. And most are not. And many of those that are accredited produce wonderful wines.

Grape growing and wine production were introduced to the area by the ancient Romans and it is said that the legendary spiced Vinos de Amandi were made here and shipped to Rome, along with the lampreys fished out of the river Miño, to be served at the table of the emperor. The Amandi area in the Sil valley today produces some of the region's best wines.

Also with January's pruning comes the work of clearing the weeds and vine shoots that have grown up between the vines in the last few months. The clearing used to be done by digging by hand between the vines, but now it's done with machines; small tillers, and brush cutters or, unfortunately, increasingly with herbicide. Today many of the owners of small vineyards, particularly the younger owners, live in larger nearby towns, and for them spraying herbicide is a way to do in an hour or two a job that might otherwise take a day or two. And in larger vineyards it saves many hours of labour that must be paid for. But many local winegrowers disapprove of it.

Once the initial clearing and pruning are done, there is a pause in activity until the vines flower. The flowering occurs in late April or early May. Grapevines have little need for bees or insects, as their flowers are usually hermaphroditic, what are called perfect flowers, which can self-pollinate. The flowers are tiny and green and barely noticeable. The cycle of the grape's life from the flowering of the vine to the ripening of the fruit will vary in length with the weather, and the activity of caring for the vines will also vary. Dry weather or heavy rains will affect not only the growth of the grapes but also the times and frequency for clearing between the vines and later for spraying with fungicide.

The Ribeira Sacra is said to take its name from the eighteen monasteries and hermitages that were founded along the then often-inaccessible river valleys in the early Middle Ages—between the eighth and twelfth centuries. It is also said to have been the monks in those monasteries who replanted the vineyards for their own consumption and maintained the grape-growing and wine-producing tradition up to modern times. One of the best surviving examples of these monasteries is San Estevo de Ribas de Miño, which sits high above the river Miño on the road to Lalín (www.turismo.gal/ficha-recurso?cod_rec=15683).

This is a romantic story, but the area has been occupied continuously from Neolithic times and is home to the remains of pre-Roman Celtic villages. And it would be strange if the Romans did not leave some knowledge of grape growing and winemaking behind with the local communities.

Nestling in sheltered valleys, rooted in the rich soils and fuelled by the heat of summer, the grapes grow rapidly. Regular spraying with fungicide, often still the natural copper sulphate, is necessary to ensure the grapes flourish. In some years the wild vines will grow bunches of tiny grapes in abundance but in other years the wild unsprayed vines will produce nothing. Fungus is a serious problem in the region. Some vineyards spray by the cycles of the moon and others do not, and sometimes spraying more often will not achieve as much as a neighbour's less frequent spraying. In the steep twisting valleys growing conditions can vary in short distances, and in hard years production can also vary considerably. Localised intense hailstorms and unexpected frosts can also occur to ravage crops in an area.

But in most years the Ribeira Sacra is generous to its wine growers, and by August the vines will be laden with large, firm bunches of fruit. A final cutting back of the excess foliage by some growers will add a bit more to the size and flavour of the grapes and make the picking easier, but not many do it.

All the grapes in the Ribeira Sacre are harvested by hand, each cluster cut carefully from the vine and placed in a plastic crate or bucket. Not so many years ago these were still special baskets made of woven strips of wood and shaped to fit snugly on the shoulders, but with the rim projecting over a man's head, making it easy to grasp. When the crates are full, which will be over twenty kilos of grapes, they will be carried on a man's shoulders, sometimes directly to the crusher, but usually carried to the place where they are to be collected and loaded onto a boat or a trailer or tractor for transport to the bodega or winery. In larger vineyards on the steep slopes the baskets are carried to the rails, which take the full crates down the slope.

In vineyards that are certified for Denominatión production, the time to begin the harvest is decided by the controlling body based on testing of the grapes, and the day decided on will be a guide for the start of the harvest for everyone, accredited or not, who is harvesting in the area.

Finally, somewhere between late August and early October, the vineyards come alive for the harvest. In the days before crates and buckets for the grapes are set ready in large vineyards, pallets and empty trailers are parked on whatever available parking area is nearby, and family and friends prepare themselves. Early in the morning on weekends normally empty roads are now full of cars driving out of the nearby towns and cities. Most are full of people, some pull covered trailers. Vendimia has begun.

The harvest is known as Vendimia. It is not just about picking grapes, though that is why it exists, it is about families and friends coming together to work from early morning til midafternoon and then, tired from a day bent over in the heat and carrying the full, heavy baskets of grapes up and down steep paths, gathering together in the small bodegas in the vineyards or nearby in someone's home for a meal. Grandmothers and mothers and children who are too old or too young to help in the harvest will have cooked for much of the morning, ready for the hungry grape pickers to come in and eat. In a small vineyard the picking may only be for a day and will end with the meal. It will be a large meal, with several courses of traditional Galician food, and their own wine and homemade brandies, a meal that is a celebration that goes into the late afternoon. After the meal there may be some work done, but it is not necessary.

Vineyards on the Banks of the Sil

In a large vineyard the workers and their families will be invited to a fiesta after the harvest is finished, a fiesta that will begin with a large lunch and go into the night, possibly moving to a local café before the last worker finally surrenders to the need to sleep.

But wait, Vendimia may be the end of the grape growing season, but in the days and weeks that follow, it will be the winemakers' time to make the wine, and the winemaking season will have begun in the bodegas and wineries, large and small.

~

Note: Camino is the Spanish term for a public road or pathway, but it can also mean a route, journey, or way. The Camino de Santiago is one of the names for the pilgrim route/journey/way that culminates at the burial site of the remains of the biblical apostle St James in the Catedral de Santiago de Compostela in Santiago de Compostela, the capital of Galicia. The pilgrim route dates from the ninth century and the cathedral was consecrated in 1211.

Extract from: The Camino de Santiago: A Sinner's Guide

by Eddie Rock

Eddie Rock walked the Camino de Santiago - French Route in 2013. The result was "The Camino de Santiago: A Sinners Guide" which is also available in Spanish as well as English. The following is an extract from his book.

Ruitelán to Triacastella:
A Modern Miracle

I open my eyes and a smile forms on my lips. I somehow feel refreshed, rejuvenated, and alive, but I daren't tempt fate.

I swing my legs out of bed and stand to attention. So far so good, and I can't feel any pain. I begin with a slow march on the spot, followed by a short stroll around the bedroom and a hop, skip, and jump.

'The pain has totally gone. I can't believe it! It's a miracle. Phone the Pope. I'm cured!' I shout and break into a jolly song. I must find Luis and shake his healing hand.

Downstairs Carlos is up early, laughing and joking with everyone, even at this unearthly hour. He points to my legs with a whisper. 'All gone?'

'All gone, man.' I laugh.

'Good, good,' he laughs. 'Nada, Nada.'

'Where's Luis?' I ask Carlos. 'I've got to thank him, I still can't believe it!'

'He's still in bed,' he says.

'Well, can you please thank him for me?'

'Nada, nada,' he says, waving me off down the road.

* * * *

So I leave the miraculous village of Ruitelan behind me with a spring in my step. I'm buzzing on life as free as a bird. There's just no stopping Eddie Rock! 'Yeeeehaaaaaaaar!' I'm upbeat for the first time in a long time. Maybe I should have spent a few more days in Ruitelan to see if the guys can fix the many flaws in my character.

'Oh Baby, there ain't no mountain high enough, ain't no valley low enough, ain't no river wide enough, to keep me from getting to you babe!'

Even my repetitive song syndrome is getting better.

Old farmers bid me good tidings through a shroud of Ducados smoke and cow shit paves the way through each ancient village I pass through. Eventually, the hot sun breaks through as I finally reach my objective: O Cebreiro, ancient and sacred place. It's known as the Gateway to the kingdom of Galicia; home to the city of Santiago de Compostela and the shrine of St. James.

With Miracles abounding, I sit and read about a medieval miracle that happened right here in O Cebreiro.

Legend has it that in the 14th century a peasant from the local village of Barxamaior struggled up the mountain during a terrible snowstorm to receive communion from a less than happy priest. Once inside the freezing church he scolded the peasant for his foolishness.

All of a sudden the heavy door blew open and time stood still as a warm fragrant breeze blew in around the altar. The priest and peasant stepped back in amazement as the sacramental bread and wine turned literally into the flesh and blood of Jesus Christ and thus the Miracle of O Cebreiro.

Both priest and peasant are buried in the graveyard and the Chalice is kept inside the church, encased in bulletproof glass.

I go straight to investigate the legend, and leave my pack outside the door as young children play happily with an excitable little dog running round in circles. The kids tease him madly and squeal with delight each time it jumps up to lick their faces.

Inside the church I light a candle and sit for a while in the peace and quiet, renewing my vow of sobriety. I thank St, James, Luis, and Carlos for my miraculous healing, and I feel like the luckiest man on earth until a group of Bosch-faced pilgrims arrive to bring my miracle moment of inner peace to an end. I leave the church, and as soon as I'm outside, the little dog cocks his leg and sprays all over my pack, much to the delight of the children.

'Señor, is that your dog?' they ask me.

'Not anymore,' I joke, shooing the dog away as they giggle.

* * * *

I finally feel at peace with the world, I've known nothing but pain from day one and last night it all finally came to an end.

71

I spot my first-ever eagle soaring high on the thermals as free as nature intended but peace never lasts long. I hear him long before I see him. Ahead of me is walking, talking, sea shanty whistling, sexual octopus Steve Irwin and his handsome Fraulein. I watch in dismay as his hand slides in and out of the back of her safari shorts like he's checking the oil of his Volkswagen as he whispers sweet nothings into her ear.

Finally, I arrive in Triacastella and I'm immediately tempted by the devil in the form of a German version of Benny Hill sitting and drinking a large bottle of San Miguel lager, which he offers to share with me.

I'm quite tempted, but a deal is a deal, so I show him my tablets and tell him I'm on medication.

I book in, have a shower, and find I'm sharing the disabled quarters with the man with one leg. I'm humbled again, and a bit jealous, as he has the company of the feisty German girl with the large breasts to keep his mind occupied.

In the paddock behind the hostel, fine-looking bay horses graze happily on the lush green grass. I like the idea of doing the Camino on horseback, but I couldn't stand the saddle sores and having to look after the poor animal. I've had enough trouble just looking after myself just recently, but blisters on my arse, no thanks.

I go to bed early and notice the German girl sneaking into our room and sliding into bed with the one-legged chap, and in seconds she starts giggling.

Triacastella to Portomarin:
Pablo Coolio 1 Germany 0

An epic 9:00 a.m. lie in, followed by coffee and toast in the café. I feel happy and on top of the world. 'There Must Be an Angel' by the Eurythmics is playing on MTV, and I resign myself to the fact that I still have no hope in hell of mastering the Stevie Wonder harmonica solo in a million years. I could quite happily sit here all day, deep in contemplation, but the wheels of steel are already in motion. According to Swiss John's theory, these last few kilometers are where I should be reflecting and wondering how to live the final chapters of my life, but the thought of returning to Scunthorpe fills me with dread.

On the outskirts of Sarria I see the two very familiar figures of Dr. Andreas and Greta resting at a bridge. They are amazed to see me again and the good doctor is even more amazed that I'm fully recovered. They laugh loudly as I tell the story of 'The miracle at Ruitelan.'

Whist I may be cured, both the good doctor and his wife look absolutely shattered.

Greta explains. 'We spent the night at the monastery at Samos in a converted crypt where everybody had nightmares.' She shudders.

'It's where the plague victims used to sleep,' says Dr. Andreas.

'Truly horrible and now we are shattered again,' she says.

I feel for both of them and I'm pleased I stayed where I stayed, but I have to be on, so I bid farewell to my friends and hope to see them in Santiago.

As I approach the hostel in the woodland village of Ferreiros, I notice the blank expressionless faces of ghost-like pilgrims, haunting around the entrances and exits with their worried grey faces already deciding my position in their queue. 'Well, not today José.'

I give them five loud blasts of the 'Great Escape' and a V for victory sign as I pass. Their shocked, sour faces say it all.

Rain clouds gather above me and the sky turns black, but I don't care;

I feel alive! Then, without warning, the heavens open and the cleansing, baptizing, rejuvenating rain ruins my last cigarette.

The light fades quickly as I cross the great bridge of Portomarin, with the yellow arrows leading me into a deserted hostel with no sign of life. So, cold and hungry I trudge further into the deserted town, sitting for a while on the steps of an empty hotel as darkness falls.

The place reminds me of a seaside resort closed down for the winter and I can't sit here all night; so I follow my instincts and press on through the deserted streets.

I hear him before I actually see him. 'Theo!' I shout.

After an eardrum-shattering, hand-crushing reintroduction he shows me inside the hostel to the bottom bunk on the very last bed, telling me that most of the lightweight pilgrims have stayed here for another night because of the rain, creating a pilgrim backlog of miserable faces.

I manage to find a dry T-shirt at the bottom of my pack and have the pilgrim's meal at the restaurant with Alyssa, who tells me that Dave and Eva are very much an item now, staying in cheap hotels and pensions instead of the pilgrims' hostels.

'They're even talking about starting a family,' she says.

So on that note, I opt for an early night with Pablo Coolio. Maybe now in my sobriety I can understand what on earth he's talking about.

It might make me a better person; maybe even benefit from reading it?

~

Abandonment

by J.P. Vincent

Where are the old men? Who once sat here on these moss
     covered stone benches,
Biding their time, waiting, their labours ended,
Waiting for a call, a call that satisfies their hunger.
Chatting about old times, when they could say,
Where has my time gone?

Where are the children? Who once shouted
And ran and played through these now weed filled alleys,
Yelling out to friends and insults to foes.
Their shouts now unheard from behind the locked gates
     and bricked up openings, forever barred
from the school yard, no more the tramp of feet the exulted
     laughter of freedom.

Where are the old women? Their scarves tightly knotted
     under chin, chattering their way to heaven.
To pray and confess their sins. Is neglect a sin?
To leave this building to decay, its twin bells forlorn ropes
     perished.
Black forged chandeliers hang drunk from the rafters.
The new sinners reflect the decay with their drunkenness
     and stagger in for sanctuary clutching spirits unholy.

Where are the men? Who's working noise echoed through
     the canyon, shouts of warning

shouts of laughter. Their boots scraping metalled road,
A welcome alarm of their arrival home, to caldo, cerdo and
      a nip of Agua-diente.
The work is complete, they've left, cast off this centre of
      happiness, this world of activity.

The ghosts remain tempting us to enter
A shadow seen obliquely, a flick of a sheet
blowing in the breeze. A giggle, faintly heard.
A child hiding from her seekers? Or a rodent calling its
      own.
Wild strawberries run along the paths where old women
      once trod
A shutter lays decaying, paint peeling on a patch where
      once grew
A family's pride, the vine forcing slight timbers to splinter
      and concede.

~

About the Authors

Robin Hillard

Robin grew up in the Western Australian goldfields and has spent many years living in provincial cities and country towns of varying sizes during a career spent teaching in Australia, England, and Canada.

She has now settled, with her husband, in Toowoomba, also known as the "Garden City" of Queensland. It is also well served with antique shops—providing the inspiration for her Archie's Antiques series of books—while Robin's own fertile mind and interest in the strange and curious have created "Archie's Antiques Mystery Puzzles."

Toowoomba also provides the basis for the Australian town of Ridgeway, which features in her murder mystery/cozy novel "Ridgeway Murder."

You can read more about Robin at the CyberworldPublishing.com website.

J. P. Vincent

J. P. Vincent is the penname of Jacqueline Suffolk. A bubbly British blonde, Jacqueline now lives in Galicia, with her sainted partner, John. They share life with a Galician cat called Freddie who was found living, with his mum, under their roof. They spend their time renovating their old stone house, rebuilding barns, and also 200 meters of dry stone walling, which to date they've completed about a tenth of. They also have half a mountain to do something with when they run out of other things to do.

Jacqueline loves to travel. She and John spent many years touring Europe in their motorhome, La Gorda, and she loves to write about travelling. Her bus route No.83 article is in the latest edition of the Bradt Travel Guide "Bus Pass Britain." She is also a consultant for Motorhome Monthly Magazine (MMM) where her remit is to answer queries regarding motorhome travel in northern Spain and Portugal.

Olivia Stowe

Olivia is a published author under different names and in other dimensions of fiction and non-fiction and lives quietly in a university town with an indulgent spouse.

She is the author of the best selling Charlotte Diamond Mystery Series.

You can find Olivia at CyberworldPublishing.com.

Eddie Rock

After walking the Camino, and following a brief spell in Amsterdam, Eddie returned to England, where in 2003, he began to write "The Camino de Santiago: A Sinners Guide". He finished it in 2011, and wanting to escape England returned to Galicia. It was time to move forward on to a more peaceful and healthy way of existence.

Eddie now lives deep in a wooded valley in a Mongolian yurt. He has his own well and solar electricity. Eddie would love to write again someday, but he has a ruined house to restore, a ruined body and mind to restore, a log cabin to finish, a forest of chestnut trees to plant, a carving to carve, a language to learn, a garden to grow, and a love to pursue.

So, yes, the Camino de Santiago most definitely changed Eddie's life for the better, although it took him a long time to realise it.

Stephen Bush

An Australian from various parts of Australia, Stephen currently lives in southern Europe. He works in publishing and writes, and his writing has been published often under other names. He regularly writes about dogs.

Prior to moving to Europe he had lived on the east coast of Australia, and for some years in Darwin. He has traveled extensively in northern Australia where he worked as an accountant. He likes the wide-open spaces. He also has too many dogs living in his house.

Steve Kessel

Steve regards himself as a citizen of the global village and enjoys living in the less inhabited parts of it. He generally co-writes with his long term partner, but occasionally writes alone.

~

Other Books from Cyberworld Publishing

All books, except Olivia's "Bundles" and "Seasonal Specials",
are available in paperback and e-book.

Stephen Bush
The Good Life in Galicia (Ed)
My Sister's Funeral: A Murder Mystery
No Regrets

Robin Hillard
Ridgeway Murder
Archie's Antiques Mystery Puzzles

Gary D Kessler
Shadow of the Blue Ridge
Of Me I Muse

Peter Tonkin
Football Mambo

Olivia Stowe
Mystery Romance
Restoring the Castle
Final Flight
The Charlotte Diamond mystery series
By The Howling (Book 1)
Retired with Prejudice (Book 2)
Coast to Coast (Book 3)
An Inconvenient Death (Book 4)
What's The Point? (Book 5)
White Orchid Found (Book 6)
Curtain Call (Book 7)
Horrid Honeymoon (Book 8)
Follow the Palm (Book 9)
Fowler's Folly (Book 10
Jesus Speaks Galician (Seasonal Special)
Making Room at Christmas (Seasonal Special)
Cassandra's last Spotlight (Seasonal Special)
Blessedly Cursed Christmas (Seasonal Special)
Charlotte Diamond Mysteries Bundle 1 (Books 1&2)
Charlotte Diamond Mysteries Bundle 2 (Books 3&4)
Charlotte Diamond Mysteries Bundle 3 (Books 5&6)

The Savannah Series
Chatham Square
Savannah Time

Olivia's Inspirational Christmas collections
Christmas Seconds (2011)
Spirit of Christmas (2010)

Edited by Olivia Stowe
Skyline 2014
Skyline 2015
Skyline 2016
Skyline 2017

~